Wordsworth in the Wye Valley

by
David Bentley-Taylor

LOGASTON PRESS
Little Logaston Woonton Almeley
Herefordshire HR3 6QH

First published by Logaston Press 2001

ISBN 1 873827 27 X

Set in Times and New Baskerville by Logaston Press
and printed in Great Britain by
MFP Design and Print, Manchester

Contents

Index of Poems Quoted

Acknowledgments

I am indebted to the The Wordsworth Trust of Dove Cottage for allowing me to look at and use material from the diary of Dorothy Wordsworth's visit to Herefordshire in 1826; the diary of Mary Monkhouse Hutchinson, 1834-1836; the letter of Elizabeth Hutchinson on 7 February 1837; and the diary of Sarah Hutchinson junior in West Malvern, 31 May to 7 July.

In addition I have made use of the following books: *The Letters of Sarah Hutchinson*, edited by Kathleen Coburn and published by Routledge & Kegan Paul in 1954; *The Love Letters of William and Mary Wordsworth*, edited by Beth Darlington, and published by Chatto & Windus in 1982, and the second edition of *The Letters of William and Dorothy Wordsworth*, by Alan Hill, published by Oxford University Press.

I would like to thank The Wordsworth Trust for the illustrations on pp.9, 15 and 22, and my wife Felicity for those on pp.7, 8, 18, 25, 26, 27, 35, 39. In particular I am deeply grateful for the constant help and encouragement I have received for many years from Jeff Cowton, the present Curator of the Trust.

The cover illustration has been provided by John Carr Images.

SHREWSBURY

*River
Severn*

•BISHOPS CASTLE

KNIGHTON   •LUDLOW

PRESTEIGNE
NEW RADNOR   •Hindwell Farm
                          •LEOMINSTER •WORCESTER
              •KINGTON

RHAYADER• WHITNEY-•   •Stowe Farm   MALVERN
           ON-WYE   •
BUILTH•   • Brinsop Court
        •HAY   •HEREFORD
LLYSWEN•   *River Wye*   •LEDBURY

River Usk BRECON   •LLANTHONY
                              ROSS•
                                        GLOUCESTER
                                         •
                         MONMOUTH• •GOODRICH
ABERGAVENNY•   •
                  RAGLAN
                   •   BROCKWEIR
                                  •
              •USK   •TINTERN

              CHEPSTOW•

NEWPORT•

CARDIFF   BRISTOL
       • SHIREHAMPTON •   •

Map of the Wye Valley region, showing places mentioned in the text

Preface

Anyone who has read some of William Wordsworth's poetry or visited Dove Cottage and Rydal Mount, his homes in Cumbria, will know that he belonged to the Lake District. Yet many people living in or near the Wye valley may not be aware that he came on 11 occasions to their equally lovely land on either side of the English-Welsh border. The following pages investigate this aspect of his life, to which his biographers have tended to pay little attention. He and his immediate family had many interesting experiences not only in Herefordshire but also down the Wye in Monmouthshire, in the east of Radnorshire, and on the edges of Gloucestershire, Worcestershire, Shropshire and Breconshire.

It is commonplace to associate William with his sister Dorothy, but in following him around the Wye valley priority must be given to his wife Mary, her sister Sarah Hutchinson, her brother Tom Hutchinson and his wife Mary, along with this younger Mary's brother John Monkhouse.

The marriages of the two Marys knit the seven people together. William and Mary married in 1802 and had had their five children before the wedding of Tom and the other Mary in 1812. Then they also had five children.

Dorothy	William	=	Mary	Sarah	Tom	=	Mary	John
Wordsworth	Wordsworth		Hutchinson	Hutchinson	Hutchinson		Monkhouse	Monkhouse
b.1771	1770-1850		1770-1859	1775-1835	1773-1849		1787-1858	1782-1866

John	Dora	Thomas	Catherine	Willy
1803-1875	1804-1847	1806-1812	1808-1812	1810-1883

Thomas	Mary Monkhouse	George	Elizabeth	Sarah
1815-1903	1817-1837	1818-1876	1820-1905	1826-1869

It was *Kilvert's Diary* with its fascinating descriptions of life in the Wye valley in the 1870s which first made me aware that Wordsworth had often been there too. Kilvert met people who remembered the poet, one of whom told him 'Wordsworth was a very remarkable looking man. He looked like an old shepherd with rough rugged weather-beaten face, but his features were fine and high cut. He was a grand man. He had a perfectly independent mind.' (*Diary* i, 234-5).

So I set out on the Wordsworth trail, searching through all the published correspondence of William, Dorothy, Mary and Sarah, including *The Love Letters of William and Mary Wordsworth*, almost all of which were written at or addressed to Hindwell Farm on the Radnorshire-Herefordshire border. In addition I studied the manuscript diaries of Mary's nieces Mary Monkhouse Hutchinson and Sarah Hutchinson junior, preserved at the Wordsworth Library in Grasmere. These records, combined with several years of exploration on the ground, have turned me into an enthusiast for this delightful family story.

Time has swept them all away,

> Like clouds that rake the mountain summits,
> Or waves that own no curbing hand,

as William himself said, but the country places remain unspoilt and gain immense extra appeal because of these who came to the borderland of Wales so long ago.

David Bentley-Taylor

Wordsworth in the Wye Valley

1793: The Discovery of the Wye

Wordsworth was born at Cockermouth in Cumbria in 1770 and did not come near the Welsh border till he was 23 years old. Orphaned in childhood, he spent 1792 in France, hopeful that the French Revolution represented the dawn of a new age. Disillusioned by the bloodshed which followed and perplexed by his own moral frailty, he returned to England shortly before the execution of Louis XVI in January 1793 and the outbreak of the long Napoleonic wars. His return was followed by a holiday with an old school friend that ended in an accident to their carriage on Salisbury Plain. Heading back north, William reached Bristol, crossed the Severn estuary to Chepstow, and walked up the Wye past Tintern, Monmouth and Symonds Yat to Goodrich, where:

> I met a little cottage girl,
> She was eight years old, she said;
> Her hair was thick with many a curl
> That clustered round her head.

He soon discovered that she was the youngest of seven children. The four oldest had already left home, but the next two had died and been buried 'twelve steps or more from my mother's door', so Wordsworth suggested that there were five of them in the family, but she disagreed. 'We are seven' she insisted, and the phrase became the title of the poem he wrote about her.

'My stockings there I often knit,
My 'kerchief there I hem;
And there upon the ground I sit —
I sit and sing to them.

'And often, after sunset, Sir,
When it is light and fair,
I take my little porringer,
And eat my supper there.

'The first that died was little Jane;
In bed she moaning lay,
Till God released her of her pain,
And then she went away.

'So in the churchyard she was laid,
And all the summer dry,
Together round her grave we played,
My brother John and I.

'And when the ground was white with snow,
And I could run and slide,
My brother John was forced to go,
And he lies by her side.'

'How many are you then'; said I,
'If they two are in heaven?'
The little Maiden did reply,
'O Master, we are seven.'

'But they are dead, those two are dead,
Their spirits are in heaven.'
'Twas throwing words away, for still
The little maid would have her will,
And said, 'Nay, we are seven!'

From Goodrich William retraced his steps down the Wye, moved across
to the Usk, and walked all the way up to Brecon. 'I paced this tract alone

on foot'. From Brecon he went back to the Wye and explored the beautiful stretch of the river between Builth and Hay. One evening he fell in with a rough-looking man who told him his life story, which William later enshrined in a long poem entitled 'Peter Bell' that ended with the words:

> Peter Bell, who till that night
> Had been the wildest of his clan,
> Forsook his crimes, renounced his folly,
> And after ten months melancholy
> Became a good and honest man.

1798: The Wanderer through the Woods

In 1798 William returned to the Wye, this time with his sister Dorothy, 'my dearest Friend'. On, July 10 they crossed the Severn from Bristol to Chepstow and walked ten miles upriver to Tintern. Next morning they moved over to the Gloucestershire bank and continued their journey northwards. Resting under a sycamore tree, William began to compose in his head one of his greatest poems.

> Five years have passed; five summers, with the length
> Of five long winters, and again I hear
> These waters, rolling from their mountain-springs
> With a sweet inland murmur. Once again
> Do I behold these steep and lofty cliffs,
> Which on a wild secluded scene impress
> Thoughts of more deep seclusion, and connect
> The landscape with the quiet of the sky.

They passed through Monmouth, spent the night of 11 July at Goodrich and walked right down to Chepstow next day, but were so delighted with the scenery that they at once took a boat back to Tintern. Even so experienced a traveller as John Wesley had found this final section of the Wye outstanding 70 years before. Walking through the woods on the steep mountain sides 'hanging in a semi-circle over the river', he suggested 'there is scarcely anything like them in the kingdom' (Diary for 25 August 1769). But for Wordsworth, in whose thinking at that time neither God nor Christ seemed to have any place, the scene also had a special meaning.

How oft,
In darkness and amid the many shapes
Of joyless daylight, when the fretful stir
Unprofitable and the fever of the world
Have hung upon the beatings of my heart,
How oft in spirit have I turned to thee,
O sylvan Wye, thou wanderer through the woods,
How often has my spirit turned to thee.

On 13 July they returned to Bristol by boat, William completing the poem, entitled 'Lines composed a few miles above Tintern Abbey' in his head as they walked into the city. Not a word of it was written down till they were in Bristol and no later alterations were ever made to it.

Knowing that Nature never did betray
The heart that loved her, 'tis her privilege,
Through all the years of this our life, to lead
From joy to joy, for she can so inform
The mind that is within us, so impress
With quietness and beauty, and so feed
With lofty thoughts, that neither evil tongues,
Rash judgments, nor the sneers of selfish men,
Nor greetings where no kindness is, nor all
The dreary intercourse of daily life,
Shall e'er prevail against us or disturb
Our cheerful faith that all which we behold
Is full of blessings.

He felt that the beauties of nature had been an anchor to his mind, the guide of his moral being and no trivial influence

On that best portion of a good man's life,
His little, nameless, unremembered acts
Of kindness and of love. Nor less, I trust,
To them I may have owed another gift,
Of aspect more sublime, that blessed mood
In which the burden of the mystery,

4

Tintern Abbey in 1800

In which the heavy and the weary weight
Of all this unintelligible world
Is lightened.

It was the waterfalls, the deep woods, the meadows, the lonely streams, the towering rocks, the blue sky, the misty mountains, and the setting sun which spoke to his profound need for comfort and encouragement in life's ordeal.

Joined by the poet Coleridge, William and Dorothy left on 4 August for 'a very pleasant tour along the banks of the Usk and Wye into Breconshire' which brought them to Llyswen on the Wye, which at that point formed the border between Breconshire and Radnorshire. They probably stayed at what is now Glanwye Farm in the centre of the village. Talking in 1870 to a man who had met Wordsworth in Herefordshire, Kilvert was assured that William and Dorothy had walked from Llyswen over the Gospel Pass into the Vale of Ewyas in the Black Mountains (*Diary* i, 81, 234), so perhaps they did. The same man told Kilvert, 'Wordsworth used to say that the Wye above Hay was the finest piece of scenery in south Britain, that is, everything south of himself in the Lake District'. (*Diary* i, 235).

1810: Hindwell Farm: Tom, John and his Sister

In the last days of 1799 William and Dorothy settled into Dove Cottage at Grasmere, where they lived for the next eight years. In 1802 William married Mary Hutchinson but his sister remained with them, sharing harmoniously in their family life. In due course Mary's sister Sarah Hutchinson also joined them, staying on and off for 30 years. People thought William very fortunate to have three women caring for him and living happily together.

But Mary and Sarah were concerned about their brother, Tom Hutchinson. After farming in various places he was now just using his horses to convey other people's goods across the Pennines. And their cousin John Monkhouse, to whom they were devoted, was also in difficulties. When he was 24 John had married their friend Isabella, but she died a year later and he was devastated, his loss 'taking away all the pleasure of existence'. He thought of emigrating to Portugal or Brazil, but the family felt that if he and Tom Hutchinson could get farms not far apart that would be 'most likely to lead to happiness'. So the two young

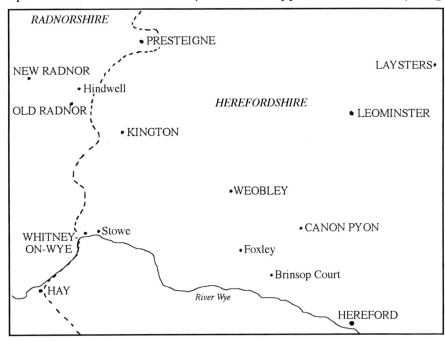

Herefordshire and the Welsh Border

Hindwell farm

men got together and tried, initially without success, to find something that suited them in England or Scotland. Eventually they decided to try the Welsh border, Tom moving south from Chester and John searching northwards from Monmouth.

On 25 March 1809 they acquired the lease of Hindwell Farm, a 17th-century house on the edge of a four acre pool fed by a central spring—the source of the Hindwell River that runs eventually into the Wye. It lay just inside Radnorshire, a mile north of the hilltop village of Old Radnor. It belonged to Mr. Lewis at nearby Harpton Court, whose little son was destined to become Sir George Cornewall Lewis, a distinguished politician, at various times Chancellor of the Exchequer, Home Secretary and Secretary for War. There is a massive memorial to him at the entrance to New Radnor and his statue still stands in St. Peter's Square in Hereford. He died unexpectedly at a time when many people thought he might become Prime Minister.

William and Mary regretted that Tom and John had gone so far away and feared that Mary Monkhouse, John's sister, who kept house for them, would be 'buried alive' in such a remote spot. In fact, she found the first winter so trying that she withdrew to London for a while. But local people came in amazement to see the first crop of turnips produced by the enterprising new men at Hindwell.

In 1810 John Monkhouse went up to Grasmere for a visit, and Sarah Hutchinson took the chance of travelling back with him to see the farm. Though at first she found it hard to adjust to a household in which the men were too tired to sit chatting round the fire at night, she stayed on for 18 months. And in August, leaving Mary and five children at home, William decided to inspect the situation too. Leaving Birmingham at 5 a.m. on top of a stage coach, sheltering from the rain under his umbrella, he reached Leominster by 5 p.m. He slept that night at Presteigne and found a guide to carry his luggage to Hindwell next morning, arriving at 10 a.m.

The farm pleased William more than he had expected. 'The view from the windows is truly delightful'. He loved the stillness of the pool, specially in the evenings and by moonlight. He walked up the hill to Old Radnor and he rode four miles to Kington with Mary Monkhouse and Sarah Hutchinson. And he spent a day with Sir Uvedale Price at Foxley near Mansell Lacy before setting out on the four day journey back to Grasmere.

The pool at Hindwell

He was rather concerned about Mary Monkhouse, so thin and always cold. Was the pool to blame for her ill-health? When winter came on she wore warm under-clothes and a chamois leather waistcoat, but the house still seemed to her the coldest place in the country. Then she had a bad fall from her horse. But she did not give in this time, though her brother kept his eyes open for somewhere which might suit her better. In October 1811 he actually went to inspect a farm at Llanthony in the Black Mountains. On reflection, however, it seemed such a very narrow valley, shut in by towering hillsides. Sarah Hutchinson felt it would be 'more a place

William Wordsworth by Richard Carruthers

for hermits than for farmers who are to profit from their intercourse with the world'. So no more was heard of that idea. As time went on it became clear that Hindwell was a fixture. And so was Mary Monkhouse.

1812: The worst Ordeal of their Lives

The year of Napoleon's invasion of Russia and his disastrous retreat from Moscow was a time of profound distress for William and Mary Wordsworth. Their five children were still young, Willy not yet a year old, Catherine 3, Thomas rising 6, Dora 7 and John 8. Dorothy and Sarah Hutchinson being an integral part of the family, there were nine of them in the house, no longer Dove Cottage but the Parsonage oppo-site the church in the centre of Grasmere.

In the spring it was decided that Mary should take Thomas to Radnorshire for an extended visit. 'Thomas is in great glee about his journey. Dorothy has been making him two new pairs of trousers and he can scarcely be prevailed upon to leave her side. They are never out of his thoughts'. Leaving the admirable aunts in charge at home, on 12 April William took his wife and son to Chester, with stops at Kendal and Liverpool. Tom Hutchinson came to meet them there. William then went on alone to London. Tom and Mary, brother and sister, spent the night of 18 April at Wrexham, the next at Welshpool and 20 April just inside England at Bishop's Castle. On 21 April they passed through Knighton and reached Hindwell in the evening. Mary soon saw that Tom was likely to marry Mary Monkhouse before long.

Thomas was delighted with the farm, the animals, the pool and the new experience of being an only child. Tom made a swing for him under the trees in the garden and took him up in front of him on his horse. He 'seemed particularly fitted to give and receive happiness'. As Wordsworth wrote in his 'Ode on the Intimations of Immortality':

> Our birth is but a sleep and a forgetting.
> The soul that rises with us, our life's star,
> Hath had elsewhere its setting,
> And cometh from afar.
> Not in entire forgetfulness
> And not in utter nakedness,
> But trailing clouds of glory do we come
> From God, who is our home.
> Heaven lies about us in our infancy.
> Shades of the prison-house begin to close
> Upon the growing boy,
> But he beholds the light and whence it flows,
> He sees it in his joy.

For Mary too it was a wonderful holiday, free from her normal domestic duties. On 30 April, leaving Mary Monkhouse in charge of Thomas, which she much appreciated, Tom drove his sister in the gig to dine at the Stone House near Gladestry. She thought it was a dangerous trip, the roads were so bad, but he drove well. Heavy rain set in while they were there, so Mary stayed the night, Tom returning home alone and fetching her in bright sunshine next morning.

On 3 May she sat in the sun outside the front door by the pool, writing to William while Thomas played beside her. In the afternoon they all rode over to Knill Court, 'a most beautiful place', two miles away in Herefordshire. As her confidence in the saddle increased she went with Tom and Mary Monkhouse on a ten-mile ride across the Hindwell Brook by the ford at Knill and through the woods over Knill Garraway to the Eywood Estate among its lakes, and home through Kington. Then on 23 May she did it again alone with Tom.

Although it rained on Sunday morning, 31 May, she set out with Tom after an early lunch for a whole week's riding in the valleys of the Wye and Usk. John Monkhouse was left in charge of the farm and Mary Monkhouse again had Thomas. They made for Kington and then through the rain for Hereford, probably via Lyonshall, Weobley and Wormsley. Mary, riding side-saddle on John's mare, was delighted with the scenery. Near Hereford came the moment she had longed for— 'with a beating heart did I greet the Wye'. For the sake of the horses Tom always put up at the best inns, so it could have been at the City Arms in Broad Street that they enjoyed tea and a warm fire that wet night. Next morning the weather cleared, so they walked about the town, left at 11, and had a delightful three hour ride to Ross. While waiting for lunch they looked at the church and walked through the magnificent 'Prospect' overlooking the Wye created by the Man of Ross a century earlier. In glorious weather they then found a road by the river and followed it all the way to Monmouth, an exciting journey past Goodrich, Symonds Yat and the Seven Sisters Rocks. Arriving about 8 p.m. they had tea at an inn and explored the town till it was too dark to see anything more. On 2 June they found another riverside track all the way to Tintern Abbey, keeping the Wye on their left and never leaving it except when forced to do so by patches of woodland at the water's edge. Mary was delighted to go through this narrow valley shut in by wooded hills: 'never did path lead among such loveliness'. By 1.30 they were in the ruins of the abbey, where she sat alone for a long time 'in a deep niche'. Then they rode to the top of the Wynd Cliff to see the junction of the Wye and Severn. They had tea at St. Arvans and walked through the forest at Piercefield high above the Wye, marvelling at the awesome precipices and extraordinary splendour of this region, hidden away today behind Chepstow racecourse. Mary was so thrilled that in the evening she jotted down an outline of their adventures while she

11

East view of Tintern Abbey, 1800

and Tom talked across the table at the Beaufort Arms in Chepstow. On 3 June they looked round the town and enjoyed another beautiful ride to Raglan Castle. At Mary's suggestion they made a detour to Usk, reaching the Three Salmon Inn for tea at 7 p.m. She then walked upstream alone for half a mile, 'the western sky and the Welsh hills in

West view of Tintern Abbey, 1800

front of me', to visit a servant at a country house standing about where Beech Hill is today on the road to Abergavenny. As the light faded she rejoined Tom for a quick look at Usk Castle and the narrow bridge over the river. They were asleep at the inn when, all unknown to Mary, her little Catherine died in the early hours of 4 June at Grasmere.

13

Charmed with the Vale of Usk, they rode on to Abergavenny for their midday stop, inspected the town and castle, and set out on the 24-mile stage to Hereford along what William had called 'the miry, rough and difficult ways of Herefordshire'. With her back to the best scenery, Mary found this flatter and less populated road the least interesting part of their trip. It was 9.30 p.m. before they reached Hereford. Next day, 5 June, they set off for Hindwell. Between Tillington and Wormsley, when they were just beyond Brinsop Court, Mary got a view to the west, 'a peep which was to me very interesting', of Sir Uvedale Price's mansion at Foxley, about which William had told her. Beyond Wormsley they made their way down to the old-world village of Weobley, past 'Mr Peploe's fine house' at Garnstone. It was very hot, so they had a good rest at Weobley and then headed for Lyonshall and Kington. On the high ground beyond Little Sarnesfield they paused to look back at the glorious spire of Weobley Church, noticing two conical hills in the distance to its right which Mary called 'the Piorn hills'—the wooded peaks of Pyon Hill and Butthouse Knapp, a view unchanged to this day. Even the horses' backs were getting tender as they arrived home at 7 p.m. Mary had a wash and some tea before turning to a pile of letters from Grasmere, written of course before Catherine's death. After supper she read extracts to the others, so it was 11 by the time they got to bed. Then she re-read them alone and was too excited to sleep till dawn.

For the moment normal life was resumed. Mary Monkhouse had so enjoyed teaching Thomas that she was keen to continue. After only one day Tom had to leave on Sunday, 7 June, for Ellesmere in Shropshire and Mary did not expect him back before Wednesday. On the Monday John Monkhouse went to a fair at Hay. That evening Mary sat at her open window watching the owner of Knill Court fishing from a boat on the pool. He had driven over with his wife and daughter, but Mary was unsuccessful in persuading them to come indoors, 'the Lady will not condescend to walk in'.

On Tuesday morning she busied herself mending Thomas' trousers. On Wednesday morning she was surprised to have a letter from William brought to her room while she was still in bed. Mail from him usually reached the New Radnor Post Office at night and was collected next day. This letter too was written before he knew about Catherine. Thomas helped Mary Monkhouse water the garden. In the afternoon a servant took outgoing mail to Kington, but with that our detailed knowledge of the Hindwell household in 1812 terminates abruptly. The blow was about to fall.

Tom had returned from Ellesmere before it happened. If he arrived, as Mary was expecting, on that Wednesday evening then it was on Thursday, 11 June, that a letter came from Sarah at Grasmere, addressed to him. Mary happened to be in the room when he opened it, so he was obliged to tell her there and then that Catherine had died on 4 June.

Dorothy Wordsworth by S. Crosthwaite

Dorothy and Sarah had faced a sudden crisis when the child became gravely ill on the night of 3 June. They were able to get the doctor to come, but she died at 5.15 a.m. Both parents were far away, separated from each other, and on the move. Dorothy wrote the same day to catch William in London. Sarah wrote to Tom, holding back her letter to make sure William was with his wife at Hindwell before it arrived. But these careful plans were frustrated. Dorothy's letter was delivered on 8 June an hour after William had left for Bocking in Essex. It was forwarded, reaching Bocking on 10 June just after he had gone out for some hours. It was afternoon before he saw it, so he could not return to London till 11 June, by which time Sarah's letter had reached Hindwell and Mary knew the truth.

At 2 p.m. on Friday, 12 June, William left London by the Hereford coach. Forty-eight hours later, at noon on Sunday, 14 June, the eve of

Thomas' 6th birthday, he at last reached the farm. He and Mary had so much looked forward to being together again, but now their room overlooking the pool was the scene of the worst ordeal of their lives. Nothing that he or the others could say was able to lift Mary out of her terrible distress. He perceived that 'neither thought nor religion nor the endeavours of friends can at once quiet a heart that has been disturbed by such an affliction : we must wait patiently and do what we can'. He had to abandon his original idea of taking her for an excursion along the Wye. As she had a strong premonition that they were going to lose another child, a return to Grasmere became essential as soon as she was strong enough to face the journey. They left in the first days of July.

Not long afterwards, when Catherine's death still dominated his thinking, William wrote a sonnet about her.

> Surprised by joy—impatient as the Wind,
> I turned to share the transport—Oh, with whom
> But thee, deep buried in the silent tomb,
> That spot which no vicissitude can find?
> Love, faithful love, recalled thee to my mind—
> But how could I forget thee? Through what power,
> Even for the least division of an hour,
> Had I been so beguiled as to be blind
> To my most grievous loss? That thought's return
> Was the worst pang that sorrow ever bore,
> Save one, one only, when I stood forlorn,
> Knowing my heart's best treasure was no more,
> That neither present time nor years unborn
> Could to my sight that heavenly face restore.

In the autumn Mary Monkhouse and Tom Hutchinson came up to Grasmere, where they were married on 2 November. They then returned to Hindwell. On 19 November Sarah wrote enthusiastically to 'My dear Mary, now by law and custom my sister, though neither law nor custom have the power to alter feelings towards you, for you have always been and always will be as dear as the dearest sister.' Dorothy was away for some days, so Thomas moved into Sarah's room. 'Many a nice chat we had about you all. Every morning in bed the first thing he used to say was either "Now, Aunt Sarah, let's talk about Wales" or "How far do you think they have got on their way? To Welshpool?" Or he would name some other place, for he always had a pretty good guess about the road. He improves daily at school. He is seldom without a book in his hand in the house, practising his spelling.' But only a week later, on 26 November, he was 'seized with symptoms of measles' from which he seemed to be recovering until the morning of 1 December, when 'inflamation commenced' and he died that evening at 6 p.m. His last words were 'I think I'm getting better'. In their distress, William and Mary never slept all night.

Dorothy Wordsworth's letters of that time are still marked with the tears she was shedding for Thomas as she wrote. To William this loss was perhaps even more poignant than that of Catherine, for Thomas was older and had been developing so attractively. 'He was the hope, delight, and pride of us all. I trust that God Almighty has received him among the number of blessed and glorified saints'.

> Six months to six years added he remained
> Upon this sinful earth, by sin unstained.
> O blessed Lord, whose mercy then removed
> A child whom every eye that looked on loved,
> Support us, teach us calmly to resign
> What we possessed and now is wholly thine.

Two children having died in the same house, their graves visible directly across the road beside the church, it was imperative for William and Mary to find a new home. At Hindwell there was a brief hope that they might come to Radnorshire; instead they acquired nearby Rydal Mount and lived there for the rest of their lives.

Yet a new family base did come into existence on the Welsh border at that time. John Monkhouse decided that his sister's marriage to Tom made it desirable to leave Hindwell to them and get established not far away on his own. In August 1813 he acquired the Stowe farm at Whitney-on-Wye in Herefordshire, only a mile from the Welsh border at the Rydspence Inn. This move also proved permanent. He stayed at the Stowe for 53 years, never marrying again.

1814-1820: Children at Hindwell, Widower at the Stowe

Dorothy Wordsworth first saw Hindwell in 1814. She left Rydal Mount on 16 September with Sarah Hutchinson, taking their time over the journey via Kendal, Preston, Liverpool and Chester to Shrewsbury, where Tom met them with the gig. After a night at Ludlow they reached the farm on Tuesday, 27 September.

She was surprised to see how pretty it was. 'You could hardly believe it possible for anything but a lake to be so beautiful as the pool before this house. It is perfectly clear and inhabited by multitudes of geese and ducks and two fair swans.' She thought Mary extremely happy in the house which had once seemed so cold to her, and she marvelled at Tom's kindness. For a few days he took her and Sarah up the Wye valley into Wales. She admitted the countryside around Hindwell was 'a thousand times more beautiful than I expected'.

Then they went to stay at the Stowe, 12 miles away, and she saw what a lonely life John Monkhouse lived among his servants and farm labourers, but she was very impressed by his cheerfulness and the width of his reading. In spite of his widowhood, she thought him remarkably happy, 'his mind so busy that he is never dull'. Dorothy had planned to stay at Hindwell over Christmas, but at Grasmere little Willy Wordsworth became so ill that for his wife's sake William asked her to return.

The Stowe

18

Tom and Mary Hutchinson were expecting their first child in the summer of 1815, so Sarah stayed on at Hindwell till a boy was born whom they called Thomas in memory of Thomas Wordsworth whom his mother had so much enjoyed. On returning to Grasmere Sarah corresponded with her, using a pen made from the quill of one of the Hindwell swans, but found it stiff and awkward.

A second child was born at Hindwell on 22 January 1817, Mary Monkhouse Hutchinson, her mother wanting to preserve her maiden name. Like Thomas, she was christened in the massive font in Old Radnor Church, believed to be the oldest in the British Isles. So she was more than a year old when Sarah Hutchinson came for another long visit in the summer of 1818. Travelling from London, she was due on 31 May, so John Monkhouse went over to Hindwell to meet her but she did not arrive till 2 June, going first to his home. A drunken horse dealer had been near her on the coach from Gloucester to Ross-on-Wye, so she decided to hire a private chaise and walked in the churchyard while the horses were being got ready. 'The road from Hereford with the view of the Welsh Mountains, made transparent by the lights of evening, seemed to me more beautiful than anything upon earth. I could scarcely believe that our own dear country could be more so. The woods were in their most exhilarating garb, all the freshness of spring, with tints as various as autumn, the hawthorn trees in the parks white with blossom and some apple trees still retaining their bloom. Surely no country is so beautifully wooded as this. Art with her cunning hand may toil till she is weary before she can plant as nature has planted here. We arrived just as the sun was sinking behind the Welsh hills after a most delicious ride. John Monkhouse was out in the fields and the servants looked very strangely at us. However, we gained entrance and the boy soon mounted a horse and galloped into the meadows to fetch his master. He seems very well and is in good spirits about his farm. He is to have the house painted and made smart very soon. His stock and crop look very promising in spite of the drought, but the weather is really intolerable, so hot and dusty that there is no stirring with comfort.'

On the evening of 4 June John took her to Hindwell. 'The house is cool and pleasant, Mary very well but as thin as could be. She is just the same in every other respect and as happy in her husband and children as human being can be. The children are very short, with round faces and cheeks plump and rosy, neither of them handsome. The pool is full of fish, but we have nobody to catch them and the boat looks too crazy for anyone to venture out in it. What a delight it is on these hot days to look upon cool water. One of the servants is making a terrible noise among the hogsheads in the cellar, it being our second brewing night this week.'

Sarah stayed at Hindwell until Tom and Mary Hutchinson's third child, George, was born on 10 October 1818 and, as usual, baptised a month later. 'We have had delicious weather, beautiful, soft, gleaming days, a truly pensive autumn without the least tinge of melancholy in it.' Then she escaped from the busy household with three children for 'nearly a two month sojourn with the bachelor at the Stowe and am under promise to return to him again on the arrival of the curtains to superintend their hanging up.' On New Year's Day 1819 she went back to Hindwell, till in April she accompanied Mary and the children on the journey up to Rydal Mount, travelling by hired chaise with a nurse. Tom went with them as far as Shrewsbury, where they spent the first night.

This whole experience convinced Sarah that Mary Hutchinson was a splendid mother. 'She is playful and tender with her children, yet resolutely guards against all foolish indulgence'. In July 1819 Tom came up north and took the family back to Hindwell. Rydal Mount seemed very quiet once they had gone.

On 3 April 1820 a fourth child, Elizabeth, was born and Mary was slow to regain her strength. The doctor advised a holiday in Aberystwyth, but after two weeks with her brother John Monkhouse at the Stowe she felt so much better that she abandoned the idea.

1824-1825: A unique Farmer and a new Family Farm

Early in 1824 Sarah Hutchinson came south for a fourth prolonged visit. She was a very useful guest, especially at the Stowe. When John Monkhouse took on new servants he needed her to train them. Though he was such an enthusiastic reader, trouble with his eyes prevented him doing it for long. Riding home from Brecon in windy weather on 3 March, one of his eyes became badly inflamed. 'At present he reads Shakespeare at every moment when he is able', said Sarah, 'and he chooses wisely because, being stinted in his quantity he takes what has most pith in it. Never did I see anyone more heartily enjoy his book. He never dozes over it'. At night she used to read to him herself.

She found the Stowe warmer and, of course, much quieter, than Hindwell. The farm was flourishing. Once haymaking started she saw John only at meals, or when they strolled among the cattle at sunset, and for half in hour at night. Markets and fairs took him to Hereford, Worcester, Ross, Leominster and Kington. 'He really is the most truly satisfied and cheerful person I ever met. He is a daily source of wonder and admiration to me. I never hear any allusion to his affliction, except in thankfulness for what he can enjoy'. They often went to Hereford, but she was not impressed by its races or its shops. 'It is the most barren place in the island. I believe it would take a twelvemonth to furnish a cottage to one's mind from that city'.

For a change she spent some weeks at Hindwell, also a very happy home. 'In spite of the winds the country looks beautiful. Nothing can exceed the greenness of the meadows beyond the pool and those hanging on the side of Old Radnor hill'. The four children played outside the front door, on the steps or on the grass, and there was a stud of ponies in the stable. But prices for farm produce were poor, Mr. Lewis refused to lower their rent, Tom was plagued by losses to his stock, and Mary had had a miscarriage. As their lease was running out, a move in 1825 had become essential. They even considered emigrating to Tasmania, but in June 1824 Tom had a look at Brinsop Court, six miles from Hereford, where the Dansey family had lived for 400 years.

In August 1824 William and Mary Wordsworth set out with their daughter Dora for a tour of Wales, reaching Devil's Bridge, east of Aberystwyth, on 14 September. Of the three bridges, one above the other, the top one did not then exist, so presumably William walked across the second, now inaccessible. He did his best to write a sonnet, 'To the torrent at the Devil's Bridge' about this remarkable place where two rivers meet in a series of spectacular falls.

> How art thou named? In search of what strange land,
> From what huge height descending? Can such force
> Of waters issue from a British source?

They went on to Hindwell next day and stayed for a month. It was 12 years since their previous visit, just after Catharine's death and while they still had their Thomas. Sarah greatly appreciated being with William again. 'He was the life of our party, always doing his utmost to amuse and keep up our spirits, God bless him. Old maid as I am, don't think I am in favour of a single life, though I have seen such misery in married life as would appal you, such millstones about the necks of worthy men.'

In April 1825 Tom and Mary Hutchinson gave up Hindwell farm, which had been their home for 16 years, and moved to Brinsop

Dora Wordsworth by Gillies

Court. So many alterations needed to be made that old Aunt Elizabeth Monkhouse, who had lived with them for years at Hindwell, had to be moved 'out of the way of the bustle and dirt' and cared for at Gwerndyfnant, a lonely farm near Gladestry in Radnorshire that Tom had acquired in 1817. In addition, Sarah took the four children and looked after them in John Monkhouse's home at the Stowe. But Mary simply could not stand the confusion and the smell of the paint, so she and Sarah changed places. 'I am so thankful that I was able to relieve her'. For the next six weeks Sarah stayed with her brother Tom. 'The house is full or workmen, masons, carpenters, painters, glaziers, paperers, and upholsterers. We would soon be finished if only they would keep with us, but they run off and leave me in the lurch when I least expect it. If you wish to preserve your sweetness of temper, I advise you never to build or alter a house'.

1826: Dorothy Wordsworth in Herefordshire
Brinsop Court hardly looked like a farm. It is one of Herefordshire's most remarkable houses, a 14th-century mansion constructed round a central courtyard with 16th and 17th century additions, hidden by trees and surrounded by a wide moat, lying between wooded ranges at the foot of Credenhill, an Iron Age camp.

Dorothy Wordsworth first saw it on 17 February 1826. After a night at Worcester she got an outside seat on a coach, revelling in the scenery as it travelled 'over the delightful hills of Malvern' to Hereford. Though horrified by the bad roads, she liked the rich and fertile look of Herefordshire, 'open yet not flat', with the snow-covered Black

The Great Hall at Brinsop Court (Alfred Watkins)

Mountains in the background, and was delighted to find swans on the moat at Brinsop and 'thirty-two cattle feeding like one on the slope opposite my window'.

She sensed at once the happiness of Tom and Mary and their four children. Aunt Elizabeth was still with them, 'able to stir about, to knit and sew and enjoy a joke'. Dorothy thought the children remarkably small but fit and strong, playing lovingly together. 'Their mother is certainly the best manager of children I ever saw, combining firmness and steadiness with the utmost tenderness'. Soon Mary was pregnant again, and threatened with another miscarriage. In March they went together in a gig to stay with John Monkhouse at the Stowe, driving over the recently built bridge across the Wye at Whitney to visit Clifford and Hay. But the outing proved almost too much for Mary and they were thankful to get safely home to Brinsop. Dorothy so enjoyed John's company and the quietness of the Stowe that she went back five times, spending 30 days of her seven-month visit there.

In April she travelled south through Hereford, Rotherwas and Holme Lacy to Ballingham, stopping a while at Hollington Farm. Thomas, Tom's 8 year-old son, had been sent to school in Ballingham, where one of his uncles was living. Dorothy did not think much of the scheme but hesitated to interfere. Then she went on to Hoarwithy, Ross, Wilton and Goodrich Castle, 'very beautiful on its woody eminence', to spend the night of 25 April in Monmouth at the Angel Inn which in those days occupied the corner site opposite St. Mary's Church. That evening she crossed the bridge and strolled on the far side of the Wye. Abandoning the idea of going to Tintern, she left at 6 a.m. next morning to return to Ballingham, shocked to find an iron forge belching smoke over the splendid stretch of the river at New Weir just below Symonds Yat, which she had so much enjoyed with William 28 years earlier.

Though business was so bad that some local banks failed, Tom was very pleased with his first year at Brinsop Court. He gave up two Radnorshire farms which he had held for a time—Broadheath near Presteigne and Allt-y-corryn near Glascwm—but he retained Gwerndyfnant. In May, Dorothy spent two weeks at 'dear Gwern' and so enjoyed its splendid position high up on the ledge of a steep hillside, surrounded by woods with glorious views westwards, that she tried her hand at writing poetry about it. Tom housed farm hands at the Gyfron Cottages in the hamlet of Weythel, from which a grassy track still leads to a ford across the Gilwern Brook and up through woods to the house, which was not at that time hedged in by farm buildings as it is today.

Dorothy devoted one week to Worcester and on 1 June enjoyed a 'delicious walk' along the narrow ridge of the Malvern Hills with 'Worcestershire and Herefordshire on each side'. She had originally only planned to spend three months at Brinsop Court but was so 'charmed with everything and everybody in Herefordshire' that she kept postponing her departure. Each day she noted in her diary, which has never been published, what the weather was like and where she went, mentioning over 60 villages and farms, though rarely giving any details about the people she met or the places she saw. She was constantly at Credenhill, Tillington and Burghill, or walking in the grounds of Foxley. Several times she was at Weobley—'very picturesque', and once at Bredwardine—observing as she crossed the bridge 'the handsome farmhouse on the hill to the right and the parsonage to the left' where Kilvert was to die more than 50 years later. At Canon Pyon she was struck by a 'mantle of sunshine on the pyramidal hill'. Every Sunday morning she went to church, mostly at

Brinsop Court

25

Brinsop Court

Brinsop or Whitney-on-Wye, but also at Wormsley, Ballingham, Mansell Lacy, Old Radnor and Gladestry. She was often in Hereford, yet mentioned nothing about it apart from the Cathedral, the Market, and the Castle Green. Close by she went to Huntington Court with its beautiful 'long, canal-like pool', while on the Welsh border away to the west of Kington she visited the other Huntington with its castle ruins on a steep hillock. She was often in and out of Kington, attended 'Merry Kington Fair', admired the churchyard and 'flower gardens', and went to Kington Races. Twice she could not resist going back to Hindwell to see the pair of swans and 'the brook, just the same as when I used to wander there'.

It was towards the end of her stay, on 22 August, that Osman Ricardo, Tom's young landlord, rode over from Gatcombe Park in Gloucestershire, leaving with him the document leasing the Court and promising to return with his wife for breakfast next morning. The lease duly signed and responsibility for repairs amicably settled, the Ricardos, Tom and even Mary set out on horseback for the wooded hilltop known as Ladylift and the Raven's Causeway, where the golf course was one day to be sited. Dorothy was unwell but met the visitors at dinner. Encouraged by the friendliness of the Ricardos, Tom and Mary persuaded the couple to stay overnight.

On 30 August William Wordsworth's eldest son, John, aged 23, joined the household. Next day Dorothy paid her final visit to the Stowe. Young John followed her and together with John Monkhouse they climbed Merbach hill with its incomparable views of the Wye winding out of Wales into England.

On 8 September, her last day, she walked with Mary, the children and John Wordsworth to Brinsop churchyard. That night the moon shone brightly, 'reflected in the pond', where one swan was gliding as she walked reflectively in the garden. Next morning the children went with her in the cart for a while, John Wordsworth following on foot. Then she 'neither looked nor spoke' till they reached the Lugg Meadows and from the hilltop above Lugwardine 'looked back on old friends for the last time'. At the Malvern Hills she gazed westwards once more, then went on to Worcester and eventually back to Rydal Mount, her mind still full of 'the rich fields and woods and scattered hills and orchards of Herefordshire'. She was never to see them again.

On 9 December, Sarah, Mary's fifth child arrived, the only one of the family to be born at Brinsop Court.

1827-1834: Sarah Hutchinson, the very useful Guest
In August 1827 Mary Wordsworth brought her daughter Dora to Brinsop Court. Dora had been ill and it was felt that a drier climate would be beneficial. William joined them in December, spending two days in Birmingham on the way, two in Worcester, and planning a stop at Malvern so long as there was no snow. Over Christmas there was a family house-party at the Court: Tom and Mary Hutchinson with five children; William, Mary and Dora, John Monkhouse, old Aunt Elizabeth, and William's brother Dr. Christopher Wordsworth, the Master of Trinity College in Cambridge.

Brinsop Court

William spent 9 to 11 January 1828 at Foxley, two miles away, where he had gone in 1810 and 1824, a great house which was pulled down after World War II. It may have been soon afterwards that he planted a cedar on the lawn at Brinsop, between the house and the moat. It grew to a great height and extended out over the water, but was blown down in a storm on 27 December 1915 and no trace of it remains. In February Aunt Elizabeth died in her 77th year. 'It was a blessed release for her. Though she enjoyed life to the last, she was prepared and happy in the prospect of death. God grant that the same may be said of us all'.

In November 1828 Sarah Hutchinson arrived for another long visit to the Court. When Dorothy Wordsworth was taken seriously ill in Leicestershire, Mary Hutchinson went to take care of her, so Sarah found herself in charge of the house and the children. Having been for some days at the Stowe, she 'found the change from John Monkhouse's quiet fireside as great as can be imagined'. It was a severe winter and she thought nothing could be worse than the plight of Herefordshire's agricultural population, though they took it so patiently. After going home to Rydal Mount she wrote to the family at Brinsop. 'I am thankful that you have hitherto escaped these wicked burnings, which have been so frequent in other parts of the country and even near you. I hear John has had a threatening letter at the Stowe, but I trust nothing worse and that the culprit will in due time meet with his reward'.

In the spring of 1831 Mary Wordsworth was at Brinsop and took Mary Monkhouse Hutchinson, then 14, back with her to Rydal Mount, where she stayed for two years. In July 1833, Sarah escorted her home to her parents and stayed several months with them. 'Here we are all as quiet and still as possible', she wrote, 'save for the clacking of hens, the quacking of ducks and the gabbling of geese under my window, but these sounds are so familiar and constant that I never hear them but could in spite of them listen to the nightingales when they were here and now the little robin note reaches my ear in the midst of all their din and discords. The harvest has been most favourable and the crops good, but our farmers are in no better heart. As for John Monkhouse, his delight is in his occupation and he loses his money with as cheerful a face as if he were making it. We were all spending a week with him lately and another week we spent at Gwerndyfnant. I greatly enjoy the quiet of this place, only I do not relish such very early going to bed. I can be up with the earliest but a cosy sit by the fire we never enjoy here.'

She was at the Stowe again before leaving on 11 February 1834. In spite of a series of operations, John Monkhouse was fast losing his sight. The family felt he ought to give up the farm in case he had an accident riding in the fields, but he always knew exactly where he was.

1835: Loveliness to Living Youth Denied

Like 1812, 1835 was a tragic year for the Wordsworths. In the spring, while William and Mary were away, Dorothy and their daughter Dora became seriously ill at Rydal Mount, Sarah caring for them: 'I have the charge of two invalids'. At her urgent request William and Mary returned home in April. Then on 31 May, as Sarah was about to leave the house, 'after stooping to fasten my clog, I was seized without the slightest previous warning by what I suppose is lumbago, though I never had a hint of the disease beforehand and now my back is as stiff as a tree and I could scarcely get in or out of the carriage. I was perfectly well till 11 o'clock today, when this pain came on'. It was the last letter she ever wrote.

On June 16 Mary Wordsworth explained. 'Dorothy has rallied to a certain point, which is almost a miracle, for a week ago we thought she was dying. But my sister Sarah is in a state of great danger, suffering from rheumatic fever, which followed on lumbago. She was delirious for many days and remains in a state of extreme weakness from which we trust, in God's mercy and by great care, she may be restored. In addition to this, Anne our cook, an old and valuable servant, has had a sad attack of acute rheumatism which fled from the head to the leg, which is now extremely inflamed.'

Down at Brinsop 10 June was a hot, thundery day. Mary Monkhouse Hutchinson rode into Hereford and at the post office collected a letter giving an alarming account of the situation at Rydal Mount. When she got back to the Court her mother, Mary Hutchinson, read it and set off that very same evening to give what help she could. 'A great blessing she was', William confessed, but nothing could arrest Sarah's decline. On 24 June he was writing again. 'From the black seal of this letter you will have concluded that Dorothy is no more. But it is not so. Sarah has gone before her. She had no acute suffering whatever. Shortly before her departure she opened her eyes and said in a strong voice, "I am perfectly comfortable". I saw her within an hour of her decease, in the silence and peace of death, with as heavenly an expression on her countenance as ever human creature had. Surely there is food for faith in that. For myself I can say that I have passed a wakeful night, more in joy than in sorrow, with that blessed face before my eyes perpetually as I lay in bed.'

When thou, dear sister, wert become death's bride,
No trace of pain or languor could abide
That change. Age on thy brow was smoothed. Thy cold
Wan cheek at once was privileged to unfold
A loveliness to living youth denied.
Oh, if within me hope should e'er decline,
The lamp of faith, dear friend, too faintly burn,
Then may that heaven-revealing smile of thine,
The bright assurance, visibly return,
And let my spirit in that power divine
Rejoice, as, through that power, it ceased to mourn.

She was 60 years old and had spent at least six years of her life around the Wye valley.

Tom Hutchinson had been riding frequently to Hereford to check the post. On 27 June he brought home his wife's letter telling them that Sarah, whom they all admired so much and who had been looking after the other invalids so well, had actually succumbed herself. It seemed incredible. Dora got slowly better, but Dorothy was so disastrously weakened by senile dementia akin to Alzheimer's disease that until her death 20 years later she was a helpless invalid, patiently cared for by William and Mary. Mary Hutchinson stayed on for some while at Rydal Mount. On 3 August Tom met her in Hereford after an absence of seven weeks.

Mary Monkhouse Hutchinson, who was 18 that year, began to keep a diary which reveals how much coming and going there was between Brinsop Court, the Stowe, and Gwerndyfnant. On 26 August John Monkhouse had another operation on his eye. On 1 September he and Tom went together to 'dear Gwern', stayed two nights, and then returned to Brinsop. Next day Tom was at Leominster market and on 12 September he and his eldest daughter rode to the Stowe to have lunch with John. A walking stick bearing a silver plaque inscribed 'Brinsop. W.W. Oct 20, 1835' might suggest that William paid them a visit, but he was much too busy looking after his convalescent family. The plaque refers in fact not to William but to his youngest son Willy, also 'W.W.', who was undoubtedly at Brinsop that year. On his way home, travelling on the outside of the Hereford-Shrewsbury stage coach, Willy miraculously escaped injury at Ludlow, when the vehicle's lamps were so dim that it collided with the parapet of the bridge over the River Teme. He was thrown clear, landing on his feet in the road.

1837: Tom Hutchinson's Accident

The last entry in Mary Monkhouse Hutchinson's diary is for 2 December 1836. She and her two sisters had spent some days with John Monkhouse at the Stowe before he went off to Hereford market on a Wednesday, his eye 'pretty comfortable'. But then she lapsed into such a state of frailty with tuberculosis that by the time of her 20th birthday on 22 January 1837, her parents realised she might soon die.

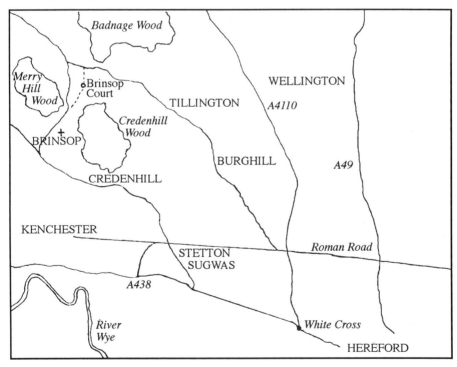

Map of the area around Brinsop Court

31

Wednesday, 7 February, was market day again in Hereford, and Tom set off early on his horse, hoping to get a good price for his cattle. When the work was done and the brief winter afternoon closing in, he started back to Brinsop five miles away. He rode westwards from the city, out to the White Cross and then in the direction taken by today's King's Acre Road. At Stretton Sugwas his route crossed the old Roman road leading to the vanished town of Kenchester. It was somewhere there, half-way home, that his horse fell and hefty Tom was sent crashing down. People who ran up to help found him bleeding profusely from a head wound, so they carried him into the nearest cottage and laid him on the floor. Finding that he could not move his arms or his legs, they deduced he was about to die and took turns rubbing him to keep the circulation going. There are still some old cottages near the Roman road and it may have been in one of them that Tom lay for the next five hours. Long after darkness had fallen they got him home to Mary and a doctor. She soon perceived that his life was not in danger, but he was paralysed from the neck down.

In 1835 Mary Hutchinson had gone to the help of the family at Rydal Mount. This time Mary Wordsworth hurried down to Brinsop to care for her brother and relieve his wife to be with her daughter who could not bear to be left alone, day or night. William accompanied his wife on the first part of her journey, but carried on to Dover for an extended continental trip. On 27 April, while her mother slept beside her, the girl died in her sleep. Her death allowed Mary Hutchinson to resume caring for Tom, so in May Mary Wordsworth returned to Rydal Mount. She had never been very keen on Tom farming in Herefordshire and hoped he would now give Brinsop up and move nearer the family homeland in the Lake District. The sad experiences she had shared at the Court left her with no great love for 'that moat, that blearing house, and those clashing doors'. She thought bad weather in Westmorland was heaven compared to bad weather in Herefordshire. Tom, however, having tried the waters at Bath without much success, stayed where he was for another eight years.

No sooner was William back in London than he was troubled with inflammation of the right eye, indeed he could not write much because of 'the anger in my eye'. He and Dora left for Hereford on Friday, 8 September having written ahead to Mary Hutchinson asking her to book 'neat beds in quiet rooms' there for one night and to see that they were picked up in the morning. It was a lovely day and in the coach from London he read a pamphlet by his brother Christopher, which made his eye worse. He had hoped to take Dora to Tintern Abbey but bad weather and the discomfort caused by his eye made him decide against it. It was almost ten years since he had been at Brinsop, so John Monkhouse came over to see him. William was most impressed with how he was coping: 'When I see Mr Monkhouse on the verge of blindness as cheerful as the brightest day of spring, he is indeed a noble example for every afflicted person'.

Dora could not bear to let her father go home by himself in such a state, so they shortened their visit to 12 days and booked together for the 21 September stagecoach to Liverpool.

1838-1845: Jane Winder's Grave at Brinsop

From early April 1838 Dora Wordsworth was again at Brinsop for nearly two months and gave quite an encouraging report of Tom. Though very helpless, unable to use crutches because he had lost the power to grasp anything, he could sign his name legibly, take off his cap and gloves, even sometimes walk a little on his own. In April 1839 Mary Wordsworth spent a week with him and she was there again in November 1840.

In April 1841 William and Mary were at Brinsop together. They found that Tom's youngest child, Sarah, then 14, seemed to be fading away as his eldest daughter had done, 'weeping or sleeping three parts of the day'. Observing her mother's reaction to this, and thinking of blind John Monkhouse, William remarked that 'she is a woman, as her brother is a man, of ten thousand'. Happily Sarah was to recover her youthful vigour.

William also paid some attention to Brinsop Rectory, a fine building now called Brinsop House. Its lake and gardens did not then exist, fields hemming it in on every side. It is thought he may have planted the cedar which stands on the steep bank by the drive.

On his way south towards Bristol, William stopped at Hentland near Hoarwithy in south Herefordshire, where Thomas Hutchinson, Tom's eldest son, had been the curate since 1839. He went on to Goodrich, hoping to trace the little girl about whom he had written 'We are seven', but without success. Almost 50 years had passed and he did not even know her name.

Dora does not seem to have visited the Wye valley again. Her marriage in 1841 was not a happy one and she died in 1847. So William and Mary experienced the peculiar sorrow of outliving three of their five children.

In February 1843 William's youngest son, Willy, became engaged at Brinsop Court to John Monkhouse's orphaned niece, who was heir to a considerable fortune. She was then 22 and had been part of the Brinsop family since her mother's death nine years before. Willy's parents were delighted, but after two months she broke it off.

In the autumn, when William had been made Poet Laureate, he and Mary set off for Brinsop, taking with them their housemaid, Jane Winder of Keswick. Jane had been with them since 1828, sharing the tragic experiences of Sarah's death and Dorothy's long decline. She was devoted to them and they to her. In 1839 they had taken her to London, where she not only went to the zoo but even managed to see Queen Victoria. Mary declared she was 'as young as a lark and as quick as a lamplighter'.

On September 19 the three of them travelled by stagecoach to Birmingham but had a nasty shock when they arrived. Jane thought she had made sure the leather trunk containing William and Mary's clothes was safely on board, but when unloaded it proved to belong to someone else, though exactly like theirs in size and colour. Next morning they had to go on to Brinsop without their belongings. Riding on the outside of the Hereford coach, William 'saw the beautiful country to great advantage, Malvern in particular'. Later he had to return to Hereford to enquire about the trunk. George Hutchinson, Tom's younger son, who had been to Wells Theological College and was about to become a curate in Somerset, was also at Brinsop.

Two weeks later Jane became ill. They got Dr. Lomax from Weobley to come and see her. He called a second time on Monday, 16 October and there seemed no cause for alarm. William and Mary went up to her room in the servants' quarters and Mary read to her several chapters out of the New Testament. They asked one of the Brinsop maids to sleep in the same room. At midnight the maid woke and realised that Jane had died. She was 45. George Hutchinson stayed to conduct the funeral on October 20 and they buried her by the yew trees close to the family graves in Brinsop churchyard. In addition to the inscription on the

Jane Winder's gravestone

upper part of her tombstone, a second one lower down reads 'This stone is erected by William and Mary Wordsworth of Rydal Mount Westmorland in affectionate and grateful remembrance of her faithful service continued through fifteen years'.

On 23 September 1845 William and Mary left Rydal Mount for their final visit to Brinsop. Though Tom's condition was gradually improving, he still suffered a lot and had eventually decided to give up the farm. William marvelled at his patience and cheerfulness, 'almost beyond what one could have conceived possible'.

Rev. Thomas Hutchinson had moved from Hentland to become Vicar of Kimbolton, north of Leominster. His home was nearby at Grantsfield and they may have stayed with him for some days. They also spent a night with Rev. Joseph Miller at Bockleton Vicarage, the first house over the Worcestershire border, known today as Cockspur Hall. He took them back into Herefordshire to see the view of the Clee Hill from a point east of Laysters Church, where the lane dips steeply into the Wylden Dingle. There they sat down on a massive slab of red sandstone some six feet long. When they got up William gave it a kick and said it ought to be called The Poet's Stone. Afterwards Joseph Miller duly had 'W.W., M.W. October 22, 1845' carved on it, as may be seen to this day. It lies in the field a few yards from the lane, neatly split in two.

1849: The final visit at West Malvern

Late in May 1849 William and Mary Wordsworth, both 79 years old, came to stay at the vicarage in West Malvern, a few hundred yards inside Worcestershire. The region had long formed part of the parish of

Mathon in Herefordshire, but its population had increased so much that in 1844 the new parish of St. James, Mathon, 'commonly called West Malvern' had been formed. A church and vicarage had been built on the steep slope, facing magnificently over to the Black Mountains, the vicar since 1846 being Rev. George Hutchinson. His sisters Elizabeth and Sarah kept house for him. Then, when Brinsop Court was given up that same year, their parents Tom and Mary joined the household as well. So with five of the family living together there, West Malvern Vicarage became the successor to Hindwell and Brinsop.

Soon after arriving, William, Mary and Mary Hutchinson spent a few days with John Monkhouse at the Stowe. Many years later Francis Kilvert heard what happened from the Vicar of Whitney. Evidently William attended Whitney Church on a Sunday morning and then had lunch at the rectory. Afterwards the Vicar took him for a walk and William was enraptured at the sight of the Wye emerging from Wales, with hills rising tier upon tier beyond the river and the Black Mountains in the background. He said that 'though he bad travelled through many coun-

tries, he had never looked upon a more beautiful scene'. (*Kilvert's Diary* ii, 430).

On 4 June the trio returned to West Malvern and on 9 June Mary Hutchinson took William in the gig to the Iron Age hill fort commonly known as the British Camp. 11 June was Tom's birthday but in his crippled state it was impossible for him to share in such expeditions. They kept a bell by his bed in case he needed help at night.

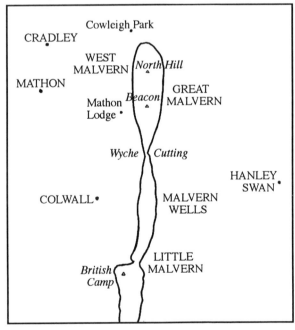

The area around the Malvern Hills

Further outings followed day by day as they enjoyed the splendid tract of country all around. There were trips to the beautiful village of Cradley, to Colwall and to Cowleigh Park. On 15 June the two Marys drove round the hill to Great Malvern but William elected to walk there with Elizabeth by the steep direct path between the North Hill and the Worcestershire Beacon, undeterred by the still steeper descent on the far side. On 18 June he and his wife went to Hanley Swan on the eastern side of the range, in Worcestershire. There were several visits to Mathon Lodge in which he does not seem to have joined, but on 22 June he was in the party of 15 for a picnic at the British Camp. On Sunday, 25 June both the senior couples—William and Mary Wordsworth, Tom and Mary Hutchinson—spent the day at Hanley Swan, going probably to 'The Villa' at Gilbert's End, not far short of the River Severn, a journey of about 5^1/$_2$ miles through the Wyche Cutting. Tradition maintains that William walked it but returned by carriage with the others,which is not improbable, for much of the outward journey was downhill with superlative views to the east. Meanwhile George had driven to Bromyard to pick up his brother Thomas with wife and baby, joining them for a week from Kimbolton.

They must have been rather crowded in the Vicarage, the house alongside the church, but it was a most memorable family gathering. The four senior citizens were matched by five young people: Thomas 34, his wife 29, George 31, Elizabeth 29, and Sarah 22. Fortunately Sarah kept a record of their comings and goings and of their many visitors. There is a grass terrace some 80 yards long just below the house, known as Wordsworth's Walk, no doubt because he used to pace up and down there.

On Friday, 29 June William walked with Thomas and George to the Wyche Cutting, two miles each way. Then at 8 a.m. on the following morning he and Mary left for Worcester to catch a train for Birmingham and the north-west. They got safely home that same evening.

Next day was Sunday, 1 July. In West Malvern 'we all went to church twice and received the sacrament in the morning', including Tom Hutchinson. At midnight, however, Tom rang his bell to rouse the household and at 3 a.m. he died 'without a struggle'. As Sarah expressed it, 'Mother, Thomas and Elizabeth were permitted to witness his calm and peaceful end'.

After breakfast the young men set off in different directions, George westwards to the Welsh border to tell John Monkhouse at the Stowe, Thomas on the long trip northwards to inform William and Mary, who were amazed to see him walking into Rydal Mount. They decided they could not go back for the funeral. Thomas stayed two nights with them and returned to the Vicarage on 4 July to find that John Monkhouse and George had arrived earlier in the day. The funeral took place on Saturday, 7 July. Mary Wordsworth read through the burial service in the Prayer Book at the time it was taking place.

West Malvern continued to grow, so in 1871 the church was pulled down and replaced by a larger one, built only seven yards away. This probably accounts for the fact that Tom's grave has disappeared. It was thanks to him that William and the others came to the Wye valley so frequently. And so it seems fitting that every visitor to Rydal Mount today finds himself, as he comes down the stairs, facing a large portrait of farmer Tom. The only Hutchinson grave at West Malvern is that of Elizabeth, who remained there till her death in 1905.

Epilogue: Greater than we Know

William never left the Lake District again. He died at Rydal Mount on 23 April 1850. But our story does not quite end at that point.

After Tom's death, Mary Hutchinson stayed on at West Malvern till 1851, when she moved to the Stowe at Whitney-on-Wye to be with her brother. In 1855 she returned to the Lake District and died at Grasmere in 1858.

In May 1852 Mary Wordsworth bought Tramway Cottage in Kington for her brother who had lived at Ballingham. The old tramway is today a lane off Crooked Well near the by-pass and the cottage has long been called Bywell House. In the corner of the garden stands a magnificent Scots Fir sometimes thought to have been planted by William, but this could not possibly have been the case. Mary stayed on at Rydal Mount, where Dorothy died in 1855 and she herself in 1859.

The last survivor of the group was John Monkhouse. His correspondence, beautifully preserved at the Wordsworth Library in Grasmere, reveals that when he had completed a page he would at times turn the paper sideways and continue the letter across what he had already written. There is a pleasing reference to him on a gravestone among the

The south chancel window in Brinsop Church that recalls the visits of William Wordsworth to the parish

nettles on the western edge of the churchyard at Whitney-on-Wye. It commemorates 'Ann Price, widow, the faithful housekeeper of John Monkhouse at the Stowe'.

Notwithstanding his blindness he was still 'an unfailing judge of a calf or sheep, anything he could stand over and handle'. It was in these last years that his fame as a breeder of Hereford cattle increased till he was known in farming circles throughout the nation. His admiration for William was undimmed and he was reputed to know a lot of his poetry by heart. He lived till August 1866. The plaque to his memory in Whitney Church bears the text 'The Lord will enlighten my darkness' (Psalm 18:28).

The year before John Monkhouse died, Francis Kilvert became curate at Clyro in Radnorshire, five miles from the farm. Kilvert often visited the Stowe, but unfortunately not in the lifetime of its most illustrious owner.

And now that more than 150 years have elapsed since William and his contemporaries vanished from the scene, the most tangible traces of these events are to be found at Brinsop Church in the fields below the woods of Credenhlill. Under the yew trees are some Hutchinson graves and beside them Jane Winder's with Wordsworth's name on it. In 1873 'admirers of his genius and character' turned the beautiful little building into something like a Wordsworth shrine. In the chancel the south window is inscribed 'In memory of William Wordsworth, Poet Laureate, a frequent sojourner in this parish', while the north window is dedicated to the memory of 'Dorothy the sister, Mary the wife, and Dora the daughter of William Wordsworth and of their connection with this place.'

Although there seems to be no visible reminder of his Hindwell visits at Old Radnor, the Poet's Stone near Laysters and the three farms—Hindwell with its pool, Brinsop Court with its moat, and the Stowe unspoilt among its fields—bear silent witness that one of England's famous poets came this way. Gazing at a river which might just as well have been the Wye, William had reflected:

> I see what was and is and will abide;
> Still glides the stream and shall forever glide;
> The form remains, the function never dies,
> While we, the brave, the mighty, and the wise,
> We men, who in our morn of youth defied
> The elements, must vanish—be it so!
> Enough, if something from our hands have power
> To live and act and serve the future hour,
> And if, as toward the silent tomb we go,
> Through love, through hope, and faith's transcendent dower,
> We feel that we are greater than we know.